PRIMER LEVEL
UNIT ASSESSMENTS

Teacher Handbook

PIANO Adventures®

by Nancy and Randall Faber

I0801616

Design and Illustration: Terpstra Design, San Francisco
Design Assistance and Production: Wagner Design, Ann Arbor

ISBN 978-1-61677-235-2

Show What you Know

PIANO ADVENTURES
Primer Level: 10 Unit Assessments

Pages 4-11

1

2

3

TECHNIQUE: GOOD POSTURE

1. Which pianist is sitting with good posture—**1**, **2**, or **3**?
   What needs improving for the other two?

2. Can you demonstrate Technique Secret #1 with **Karate Pose**?
   I'll model it first. (Technique & Artistry Book, p. 4)

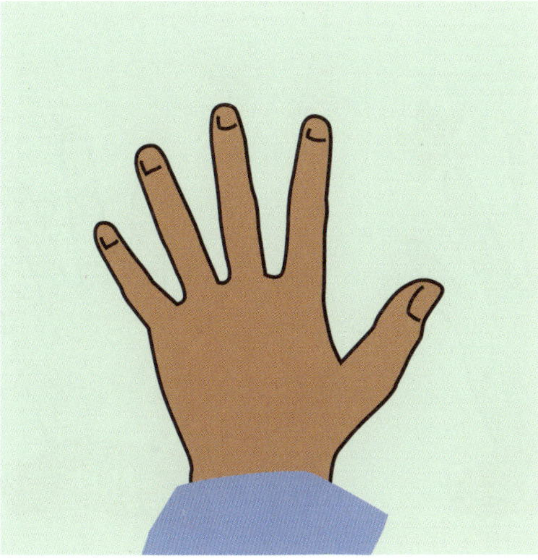

1

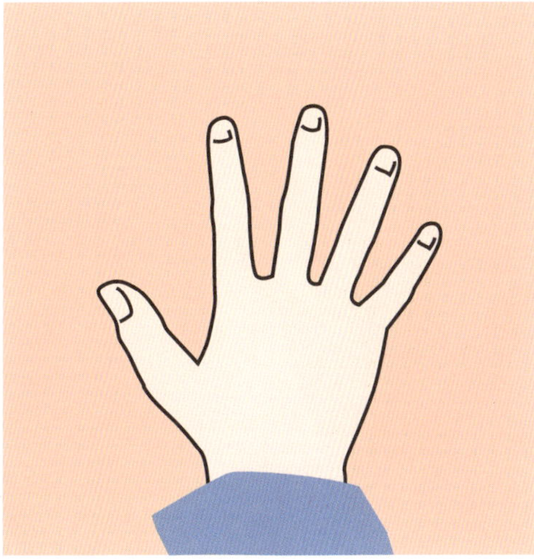

2

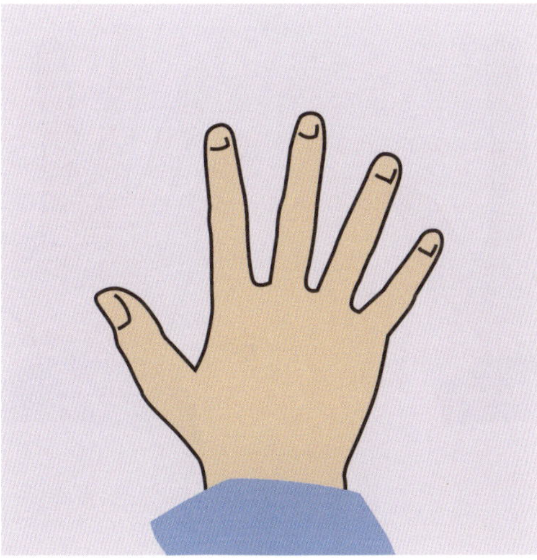

3

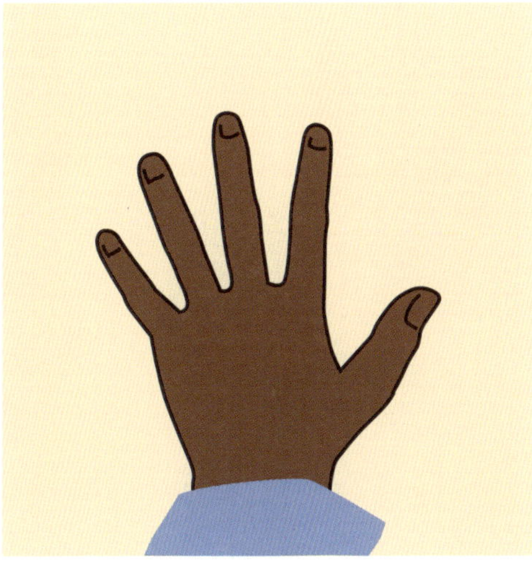

4

RIGHT AND LEFT HANDS

3. Look at square 1. Is it a **right** or **left** hand?
   How about square 2? (Continue)

4. Play 5 **white** keys with your *right* hand. Use any fingers.
   Play 5 **black** keys with your *left* hand. Use any fingers.

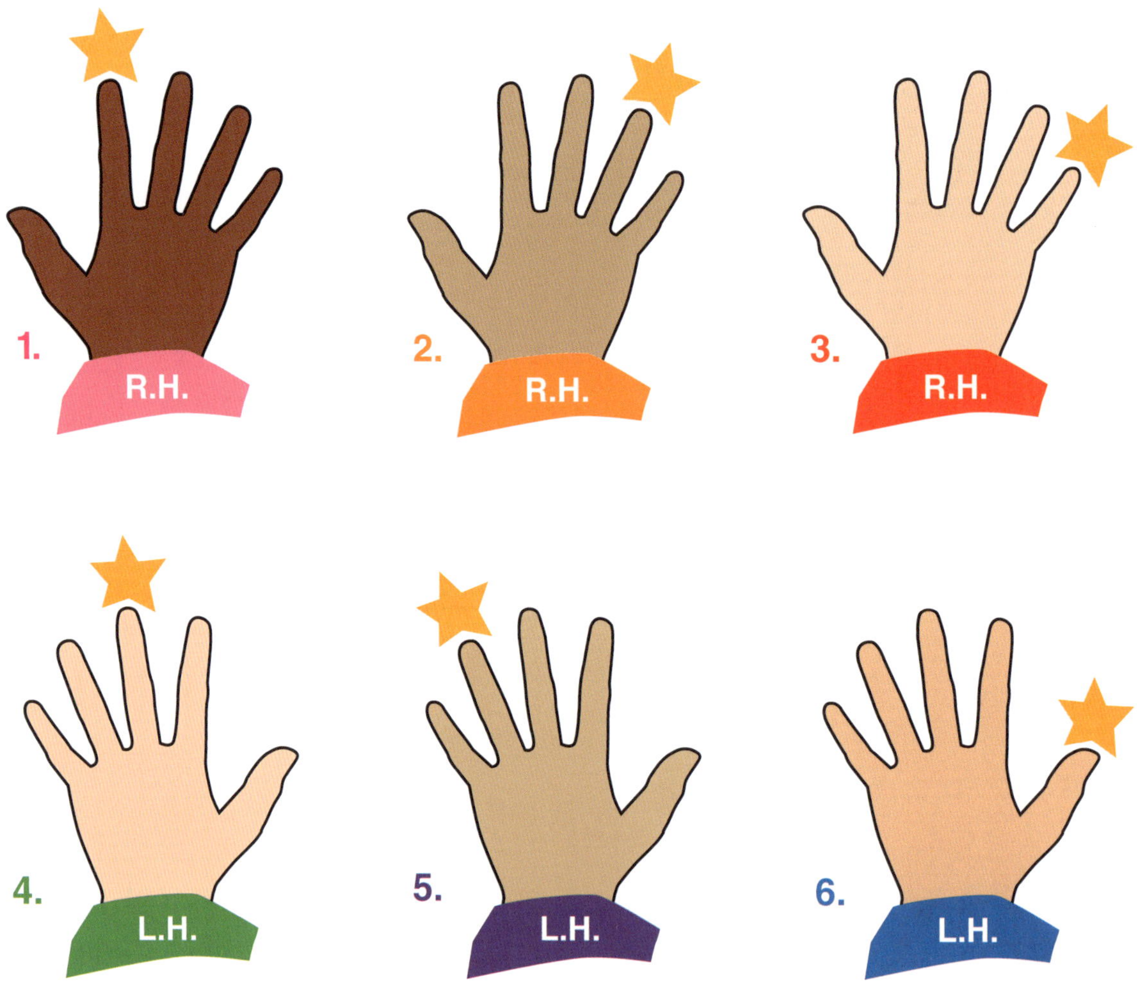

FINGER NUMBERS

5. Name the finger with the star.

6. Play any key with **R.H.** finger **1**, finger **2**, and finger **3**.
Play any key with **L.H.** finger **3**, finger **4**, and finger **5**.

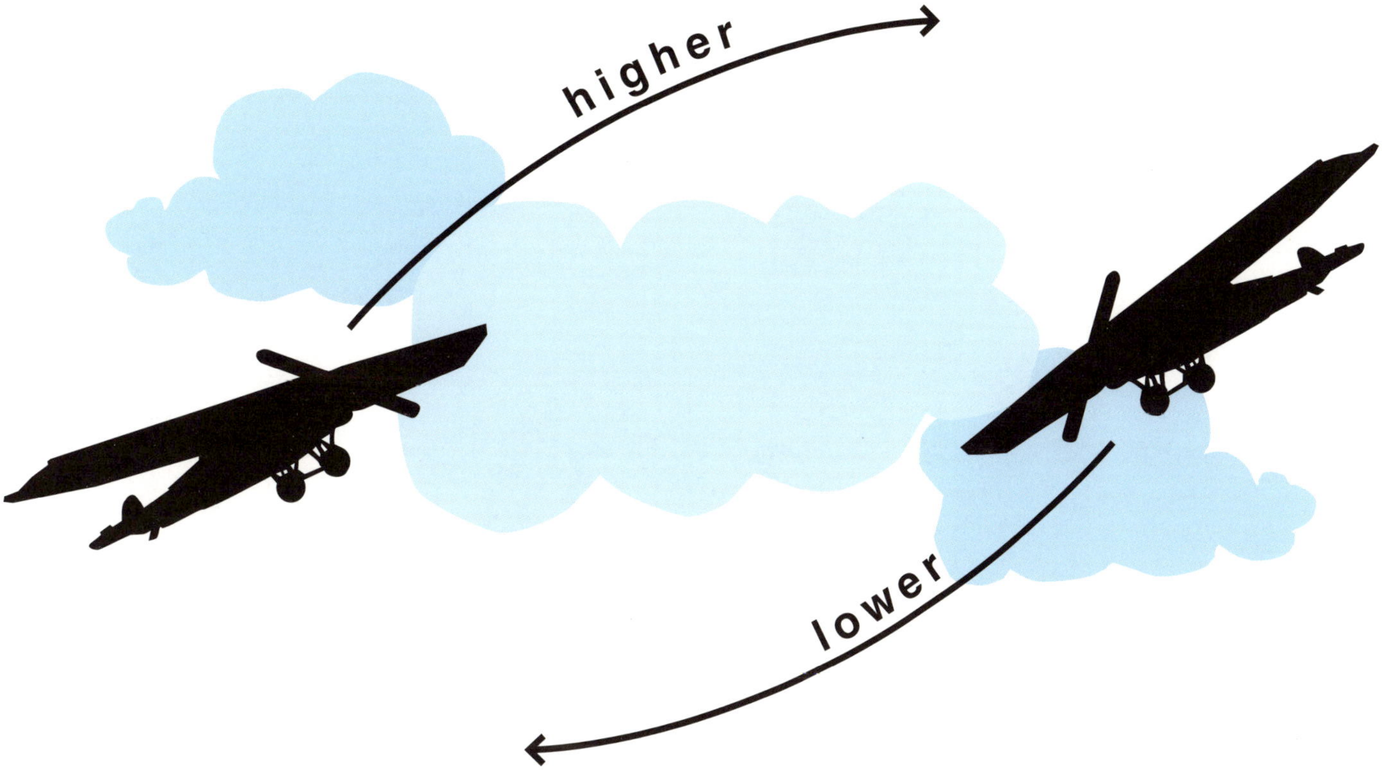

EAR-TRAINING

7. Listen to the sound. Is it going higher or lower? (Create 4 short examples.)

8. Play a MIDDLE key with your **R.H.** and go **higher** 4 keys.
Play a MIDDLE key with your **L.H.** and go **lower** 4 keys.

Show What you Know

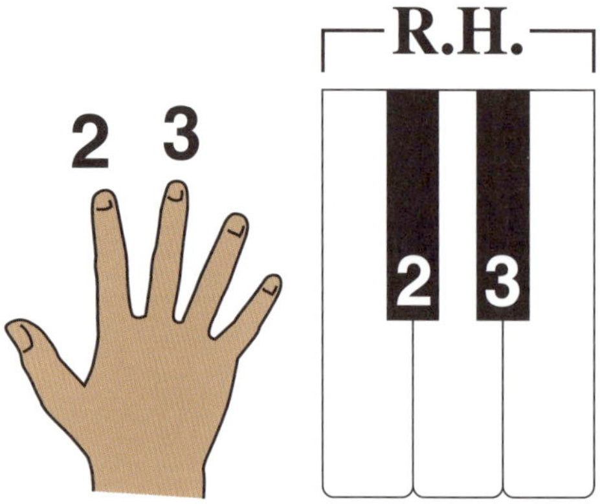

MUSICAL PATTERNS

9. Play this **musical pattern** with your **R.H.** on a 2-black-key group.

CREATIVE

10. Make up a short **R.H. pattern** of your own.
Can you make up a short **L.H. pattern**, too? Use fingers 2-3.
(The teacher may demonstrate.)

A

steady beat

is

really neat!

RHYTHM

11. Read the colorful sentence!

TAPPING ON THE CLOSED KEY COVER

12. Tap 8 **steady** beats with your **R.H.** as you count aloud to 8.
Tap 8 **steady** beats with your **L.H.** as you count aloud to 8.
Tap 8 **steady** beats **hands together** as you count aloud to 8.

Show What you Know

**HI, I'M TROPHY, YOUR MUSICAL GUIDE.
LET'S TAKE A TRIP INTO THE CAVE!**

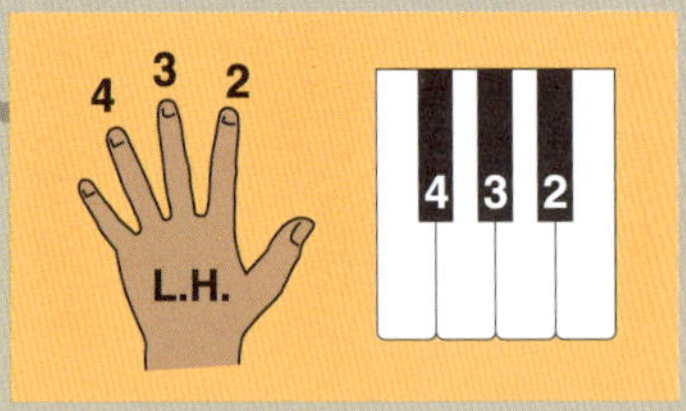

Into the Cave

Start in the **MIDDLE** of the piano.

2 3 4 [2 3 4] play together

In - to the cave,

Move down to next **LOWER** group.

2 3 4 [2 3 4]

if you are brave,

2 3 4 [2 3 4]

deep down and low!

LOW

ADVENTURE CHALLENGE

- This piece uses L.H. fingers 2-3-4, doesn't it?
  Which two L.H. fingers are NOT used? Can you wiggle those two fingers?
- Now I'll play "Into the Cave." Is the music going from **soft to loud** or from **loud to soft**? (The teacher chooses.)
- Now it's your turn. Play "Into the Cave" and go from **soft to loud**… or **loud to soft**. Surprise me! I'll tell you what you played.

FOR FUN!

Can you find a hidden 3-black-key group?

Can you find a R.H.? Can you find a L.H.?

CONGRATULATIONS

YOU EARNED YOUR FIRST STAR!

END OF THE UNIT 1 ASSESSMENT

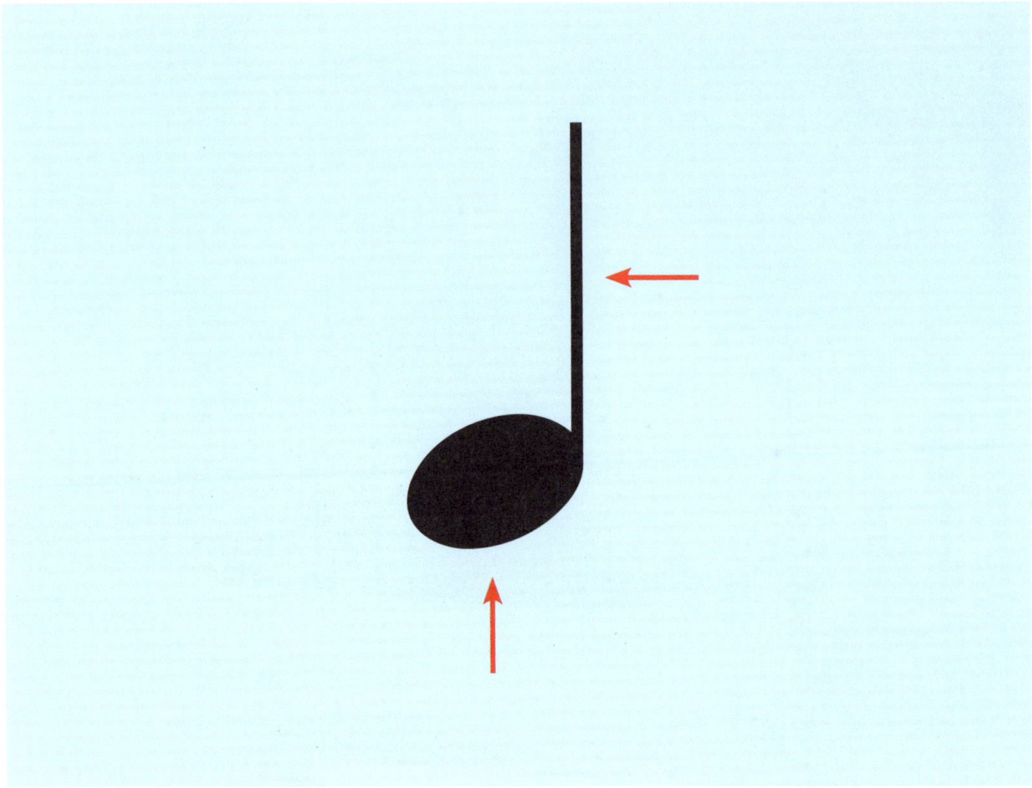

RHYTHM: NOTE VALUES

1. What is the name of this note?

2. How many **counts** or **beats** does it receive?

3. The red arrows point to the two parts of the note. Can you name each part?

STEM PATTERNS

4. Notice the note stems in each box. In which box do the hands play:

- Right Right Left Left
- Left Left Right Right
- Left Left Left Left
- Can you say **Right** or **Left** for box **4**?

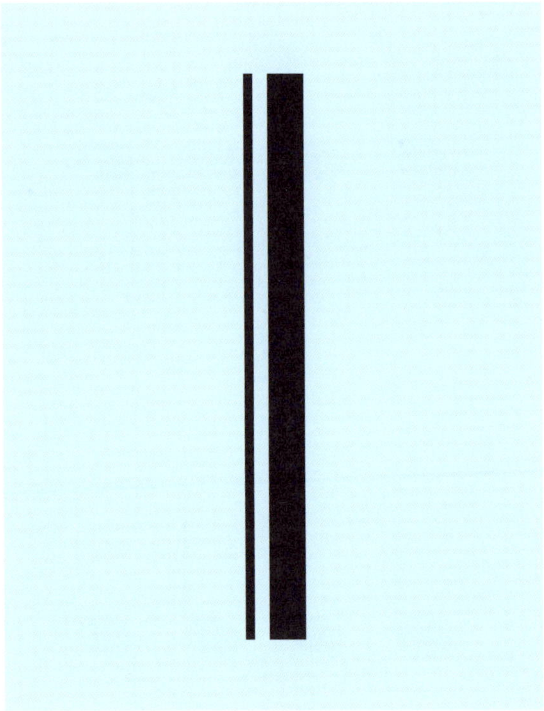

1

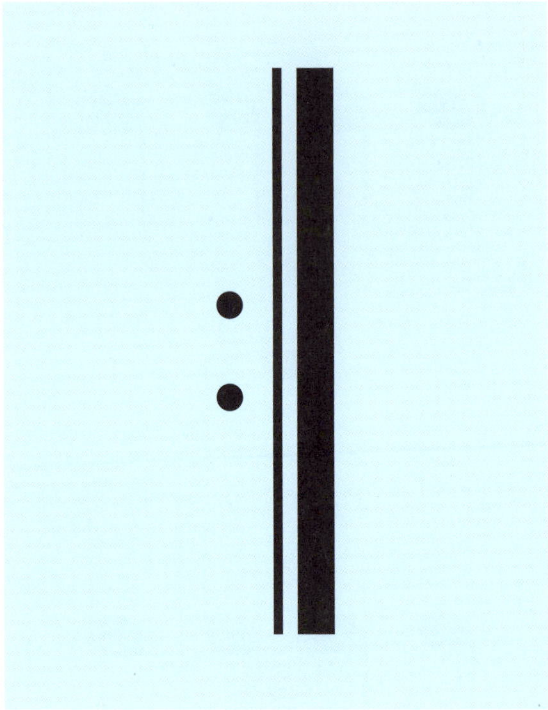

2

SYMBOLS

5. What is the symbol called in box **1**? What does it mean?
   What is the symbol called in box **2**? What does it mean?

6. Do both symbols have a **thin** to a **thick** line? Or, a **thick** to a **thin** line?

MELODY PATTERNS

7. Which box has notes that:
   • only **repeat** • only go **down** • only go **up** • go **up and down**

8. I'll sing "la-la-la" for the notes in one of the boxes. Which one did you hear?

RHYTHM: NOTE VALUES

9. What is the name of this note?

10. How many **counts** or **beats** does it receive?

11. How does it look different from a quarter note?

1

2

COUNTING RHYTHM

12. Music needs a steady beat. I'm going to tap **rhythm 1** and count in a strong voice. (1 1 1-2, etc.) Was my beat steady?

13. Your turn! You tap **rhythm 2** and count with a strong voice. Was your beat steady?

f

p

DYNAMIC MARKS

14. What is the musical word for ***f*** ? What does it mean?

    What is the musical word for ***p*** ? What does it mean?

f or ***p***

1

f or ***p***

2

f or ***p***

3

f or ***p***

4

EAR-TRAINING

15. Listen to my example on the keys. Is it ***forte*** or ***piano***? (Create 3-4 short examples.)

16. Can you make up a ***f*** or ***p*** example for me to name?

RHYTHM

17. What is the name of this note? How many **counts** or **beats** does it receive?

18. Now tap and count aloud **3 whole notes**. Was your beat steady?

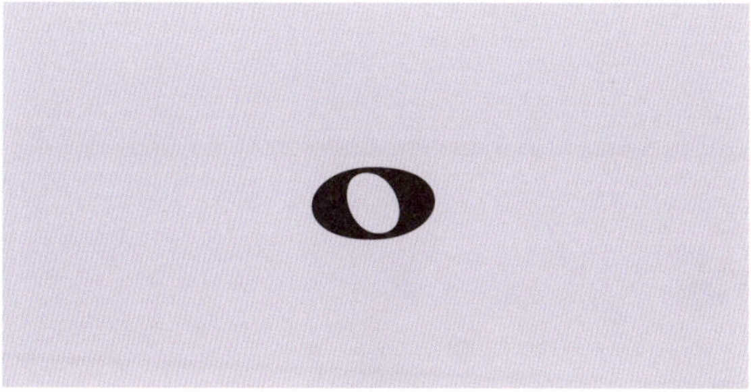

1

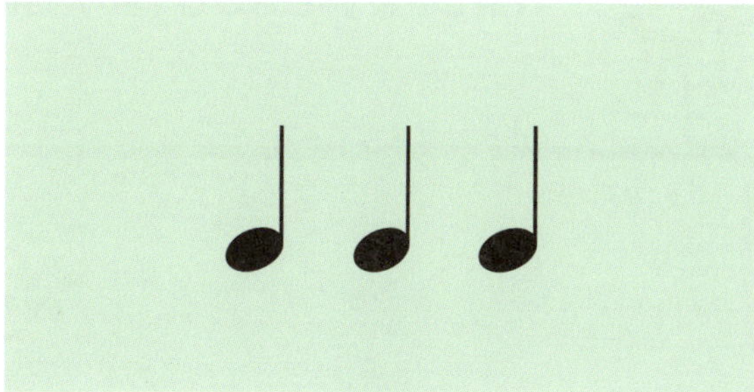

2

3

4

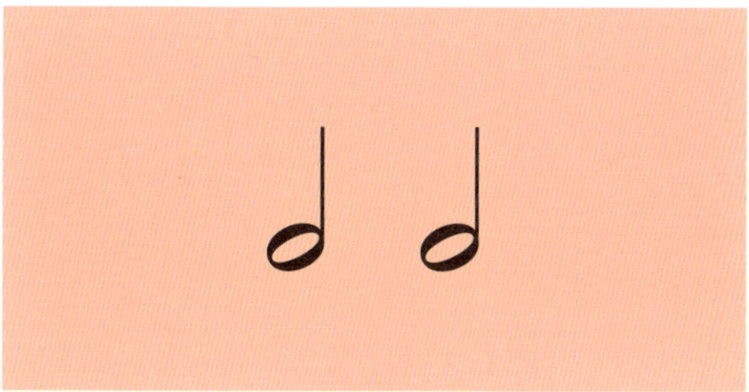

5

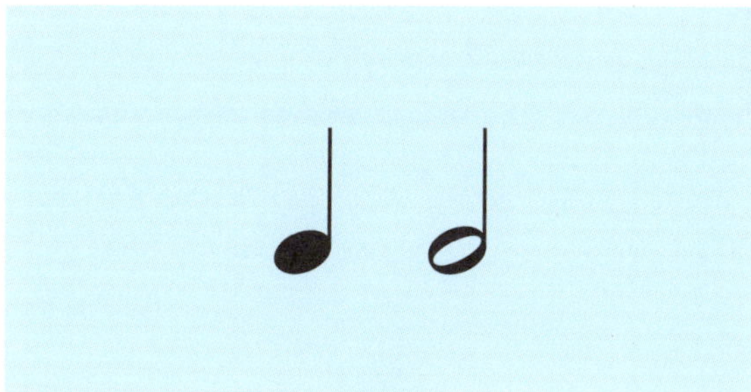

6

ADDING THE BEATS

19. Name *three* boxes that each have a total of **4 beats**.

20. Name *three* boxes that each have a total of **3 beats**.

TROPHY SHOUTS ACROSS THE VALLEY!

Find the Keys

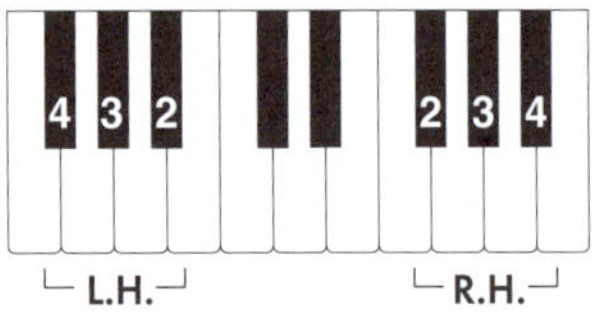

I Hear the Echo

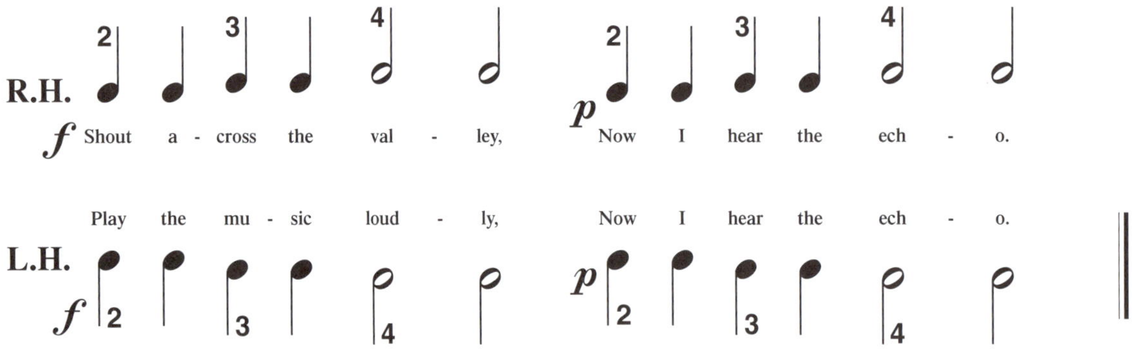

ADVENTURE CHALLENGE

- How many **half notes** are in this piece?
- Watch! I'm going to play the piece **hands together** and say the **finger numbers** aloud. Can YOU try the piece playing hands together for me? Go very slowly!

Shout across the valley....
now I hear the echo.

FOR FUN!

Can you find the hidden ***f*** sign?

Can you find the hidden ***p*** sign?

CONGRATULATIONS

YOU EARNED YOUR 2ND STAR!

END OF THE UNIT 2 ASSESSMENT

UNIT 3 ASSESSMENT: Key Names

Show What you Know

Pages 24-35

1 C D E F G up or down?

2 E D C up or down?

3 G F E D up or down?

4 G A up or down?

MUSIC ALPHABET STEPS

1. Are the alphabet letters in each row going UP or going DOWN?
2. Let's do ear-training! I'll play one of the examples. Which one did you hear?

THREE KEY NAMES

3. The 2-black-keys locate these **3 white keys**. Name these keys.

4. Which white key is the *lowest*? Which key is the *highest*? In the *middle*?

Show What you Know

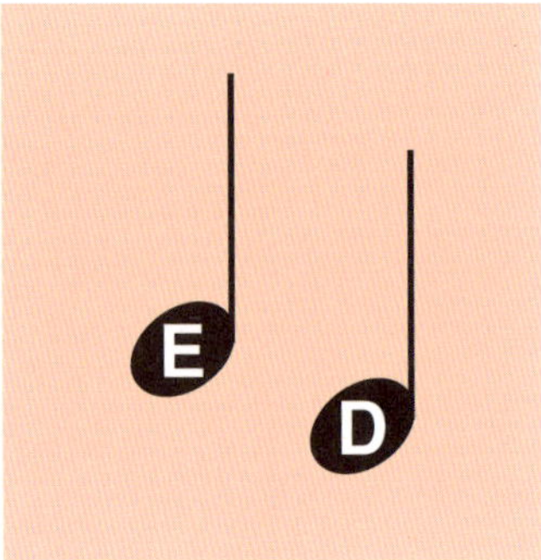

1

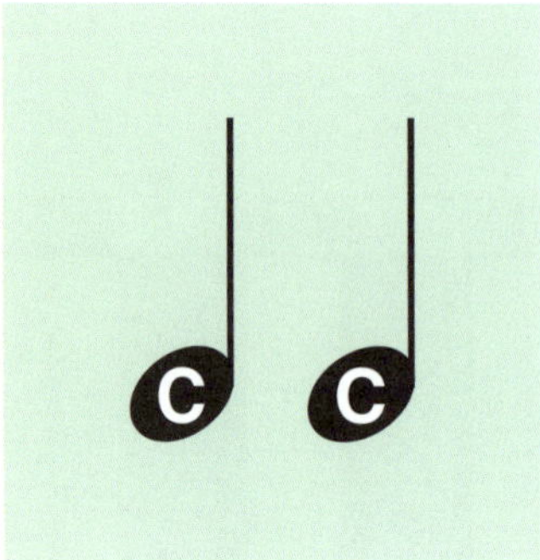

2

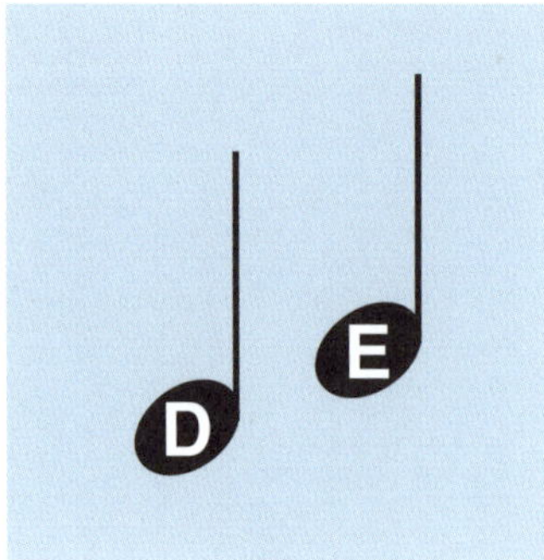

3

4

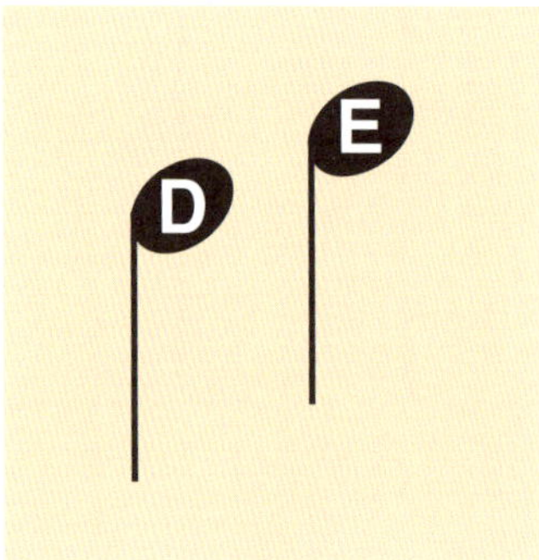

5

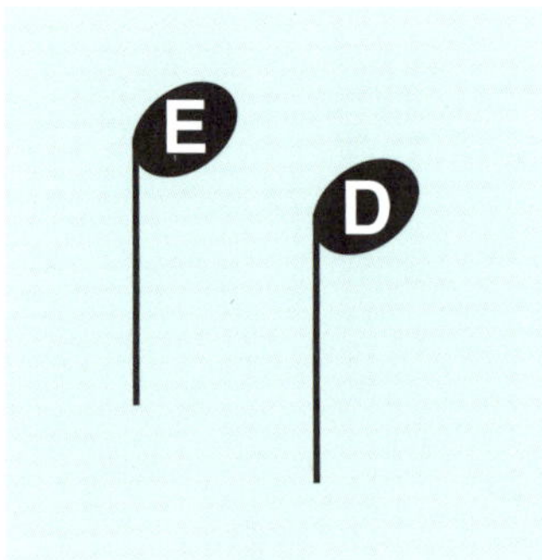

6

NOTE DIRECTION

5. For each example, say one answer:

• step **up** • step **down** • **same**

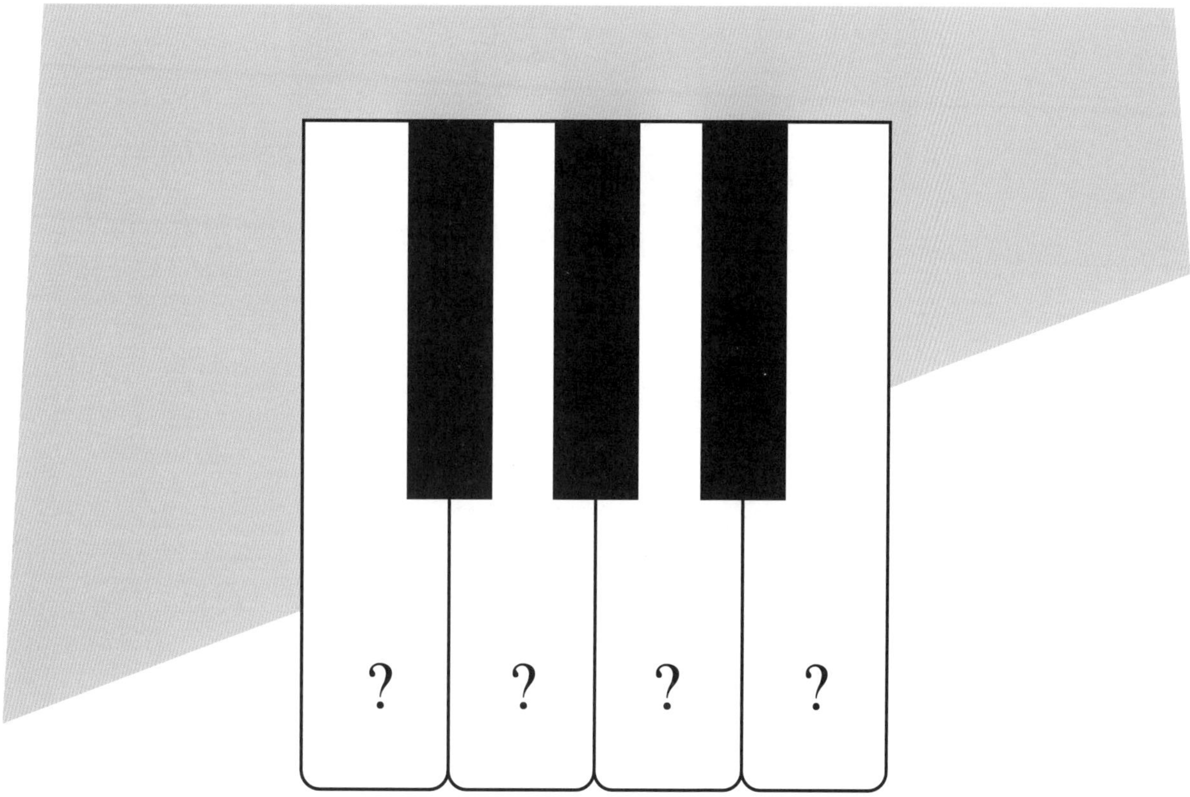

FOUR KEY NAMES

6. The 3-black-keys locate these **4 white keys**. Name these keys.

7. Which white key is the *lowest*? Which key is the *highest*?

Show What you Know

The C 5-Finger Scale

THE C 5-FINGER SCALE

8. **True** or **False**: A scale can go UP and DOWN.

9. In the C scale, name the:
3rd note **4th** note **2nd** note **5th** note **1st** note

10. Can you play the "C-D-E-F-G March" for me? (Lesson Book, p. 28)
Remember the ***f*** and ***p*** signs and keep a great steady beat!

Green Notes from Mars

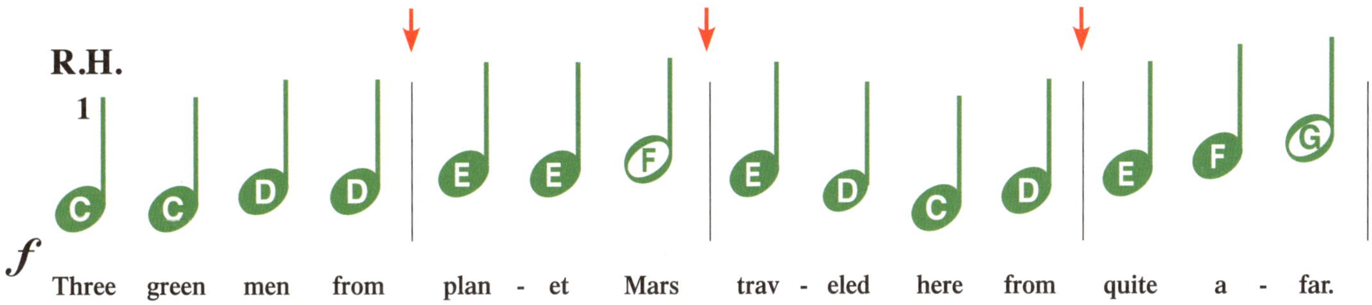

COUNTING MEASURES

11. Count the measures above. How many are there?

12. Which two measures have repeated notes?
    Which measure **steps down** and **up**?

13. Short lines separate the notes into measures.
    What are the short lines called?

mf

NEW DYNAMIC MARK

14. Name this musical term. What does it mean?

15. **Dynamic marks** tell us how loud or soft to play.
Can you say the words "dynamic marks" 3 times?

THREE DYNAMIC MARKS

16. Name these 3 **dynamic marks**.

17. Let's do ear-training! Listen to my example. Is it ***piano***, ***mezzo forte***, or ***forte***? (Create 3-4 examples.) Can you make up an example for me?

RHYTHM: NOTE VALUES

18. Name this note.
    How many **counts** or **beats** does it receive?

19. How is it different from a half note?

1

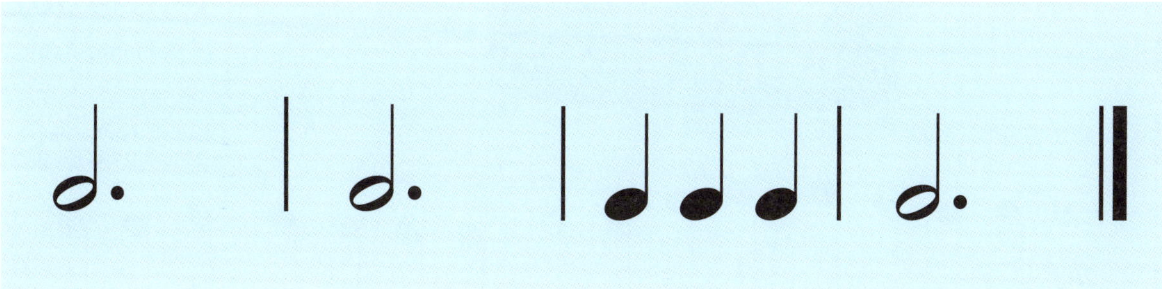

2

TAPPING RHYTHMS

20. Listen to me tap **rhythm 1** and count with a strong voice. Was my beat steady? (1-2-3, 1-2-3, 1 1 1, etc.)

    Your turn! Tap and count **rhythm 2** with a strong voice. Was your beat steady?

Show What you Know

TROPHY'S GAME WITH MR. BEETHOVEN!

Ode to Joy

C 5-Finger Scale

Ludwig van Beethoven
(1770–1827, Germany)

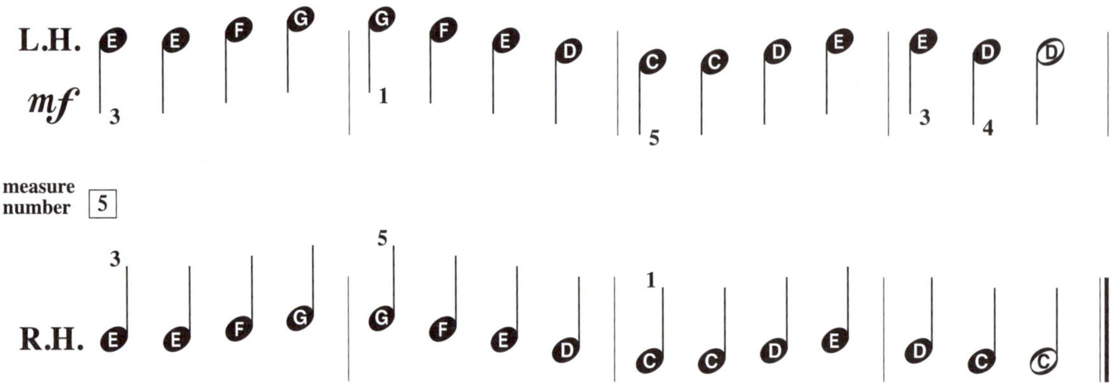

ADVENTURE CHALLENGE

- How many measures are in "Ode to Joy?" Notice measure 5 is marked with a box.
- I'll play the piece and stop in **any measure**. Watch the music!
  Can you tell me the measure number where I stopped? (Do several.)
- Now you be the leader! Try "Name Where I Stop" for me.

FOR FUN!
Can you find the hidden ***mf*** sign?

CONGRATULATIONS

YOU EARNED THE 3RD MUSICAL STAR!

END OF THE UNIT 3 ASSESSMENT

UNIT 4 ASSESSMENT: Grand Staff Orientation

Pages 36-45

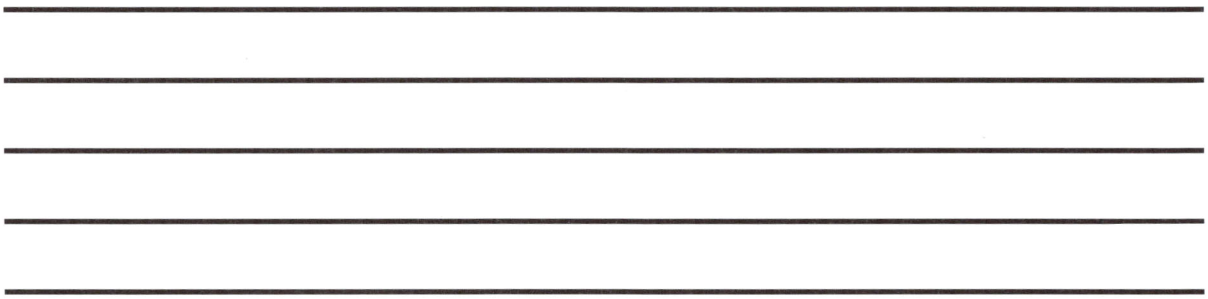

READING BASICS

1. What is this called in music? How many **lines**? How many **spaces**?

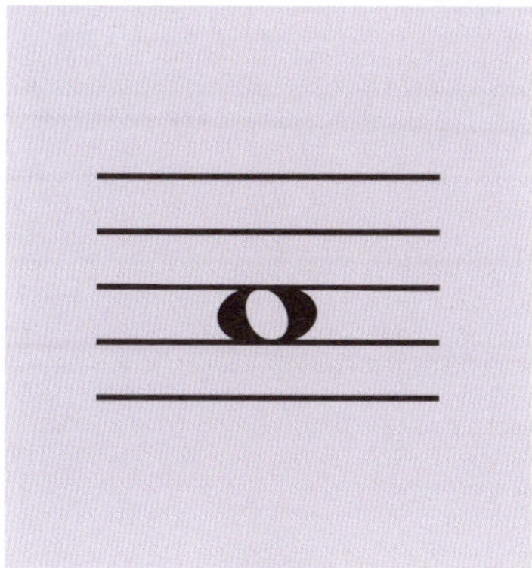

1

2

3

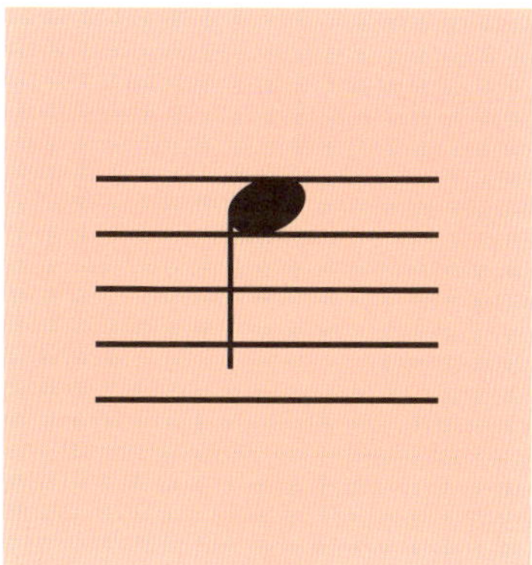

4

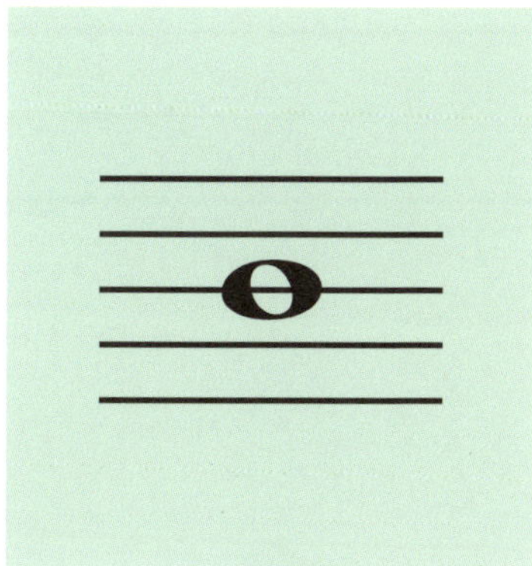

5

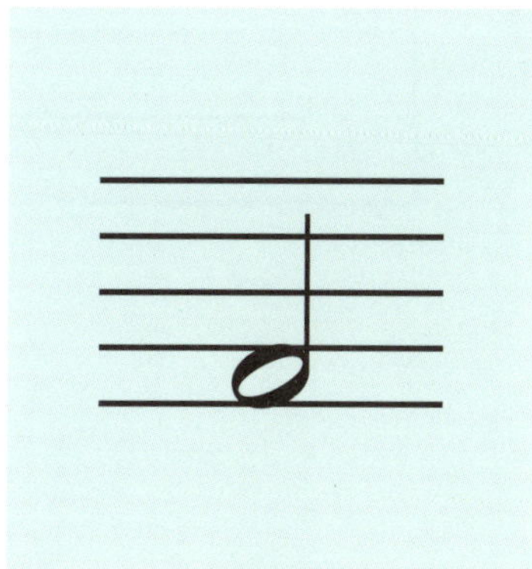

6

READING BASICS

2. Name each note as a **line** or **space** note.

READING BASICS

3. Piano music uses two staffs. Together, what is this called?
   What is the swirly line on the left called?

4. Each staff has how many **lines**?
   Each staff has how many **spaces**?

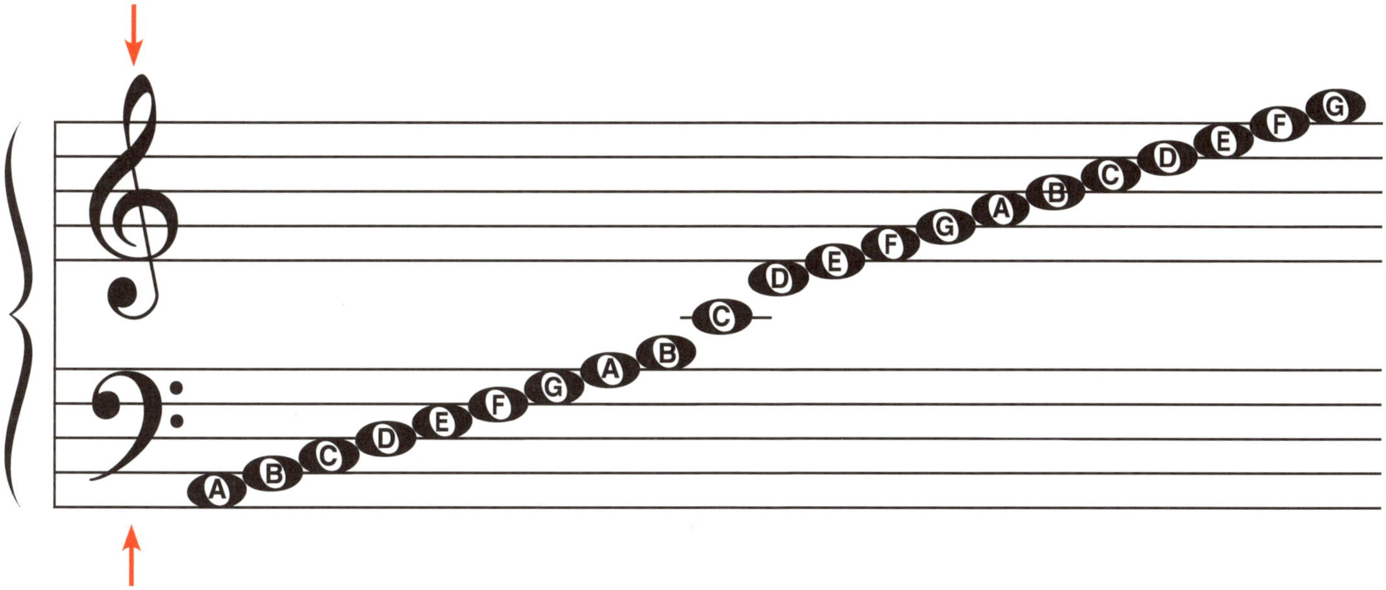

TWO NEW SYMBOLS, THE MUSIC ALPHABET

5. What's the symbol on the **top** staff? Does it show the *higher* or *lower* notes?
   What's the symbol on the **bottom** staff? Does it show the *higher* or *lower* notes?

6. Name the **music alphabet**.
   How many times is it shown on the Grand Staff above?

Show What you Know

NEW NOTE NAME

7. Name this note. Why is it easy to recognize? Tap the rhythm and count aloud.

MIDDLE C IMPROV (THE TEACHER MAY DEMONSTRATE)

8. Make up your own Middle C song called "Middle C Recess."
   - To start, make up rhythms with your **R.H.** on Middle C. Use any fingers.
   - To end, use your **L.H.** to play the **lowest** C.

NEW NOTE NAME AND RHYTHM REVIEW

9. What's the other name for the treble clef? Why is it called this? Name this note. What line is it on? Tap the rhythm and count aloud.

TECHNIQUE: FINGER CHANGES

10. Play this note with **R.H.** finger **5**, then **4**, then **3**, then **2**, then **1**.

Show What you Know

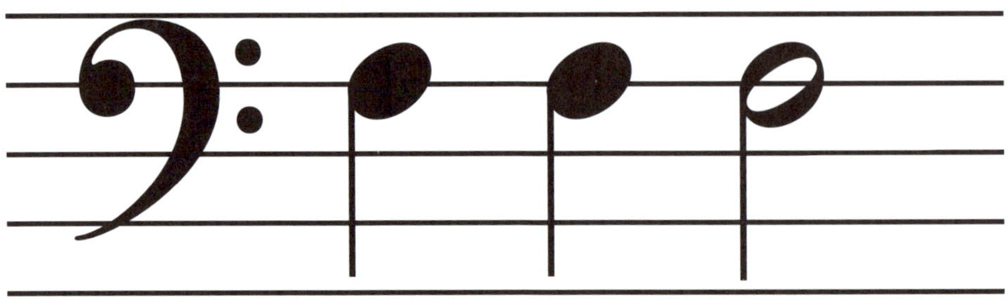

NEW NOTE NAME AND RHYTHM REVIEW

11. What's the other name for the bass clef? Why is it called this?
Name this note. What line is it on? Tap the rhythm and count aloud.

TECHNIQUE: FINGER CHANGES

12. Play this note with **L.H.** finger **5**, then **4**, then **3**, then **2**, then **1**.

NOTE NAMES AND PATTERNS

13. This invention has 4 musical patterns. Which pattern has these notes?

• F F C **• G C F F** **• C F C F** **• F C G C**

14. Now I'll call out one of the numbers. You name the notes of that pattern!

TROPHY HAS A NEW BLACK-KEY INVENTION!

New Position

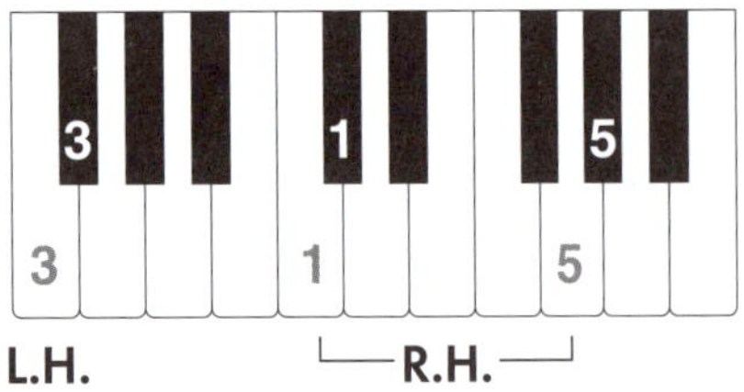

My Invention

ADVENTURE CHALLENGE

- Name the 3 notes used in "My Invention."
- Can you play "My Invention" on the **black keys**? L.H. 3 moves up to the **black key**. R.H. fingers 1-5 also move up to the closest **black keys**. The keyboard above will show you. Listen to me play it first. Then it's your turn!

FOR FUN!

Can you find the hidden bass clef?

Can you find the hidden treble clef?

CONGRATULATIONS

YOU EARNED THE 4TH FABULOUS STAR!

END OF THE UNIT 4 ASSESSMENT

Pages 46-55

NOTE NAMES

1. Name the 3 notes between Middle C and Treble G.

2. Out of the 5 notes, which 3 are **line** notes? Name them.
   Which 2 are **space** notes? Name them.

A **step** moves

from a

line to a ____?____

or a

space to a ____?____.

READING BASICS

3. Complete the musical sentence above.

4. Can you say the definition of step by **memory**?

Show What you Know

DIRECTIONAL READING

5. For each example in the tree, say one answer.
 • **step up** • **step down** • **both**

NOTE NAMES

6. Name all the notes on the bluebird's path as fast as you can. Now try it again! Did you name them faster this time?

4 means ____ beats in a measure

4 means the ____ note gets 1 beat

RHYTHM

7. What are these 2 numbers called?

8. What does the top number tell us about each **measure**?
   What does the bottom number tell us about the **beat**?

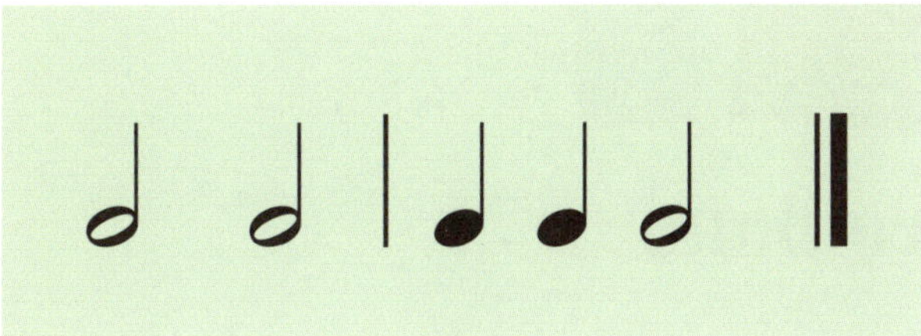

1

2

3

4

5

6

THE TIME SIGNATURE

9. Which examples are in $\frac{4}{4}$ time? Hint: There are four.

10. Which example begins with a dotted half note?

Show What you Know

The Dance Band

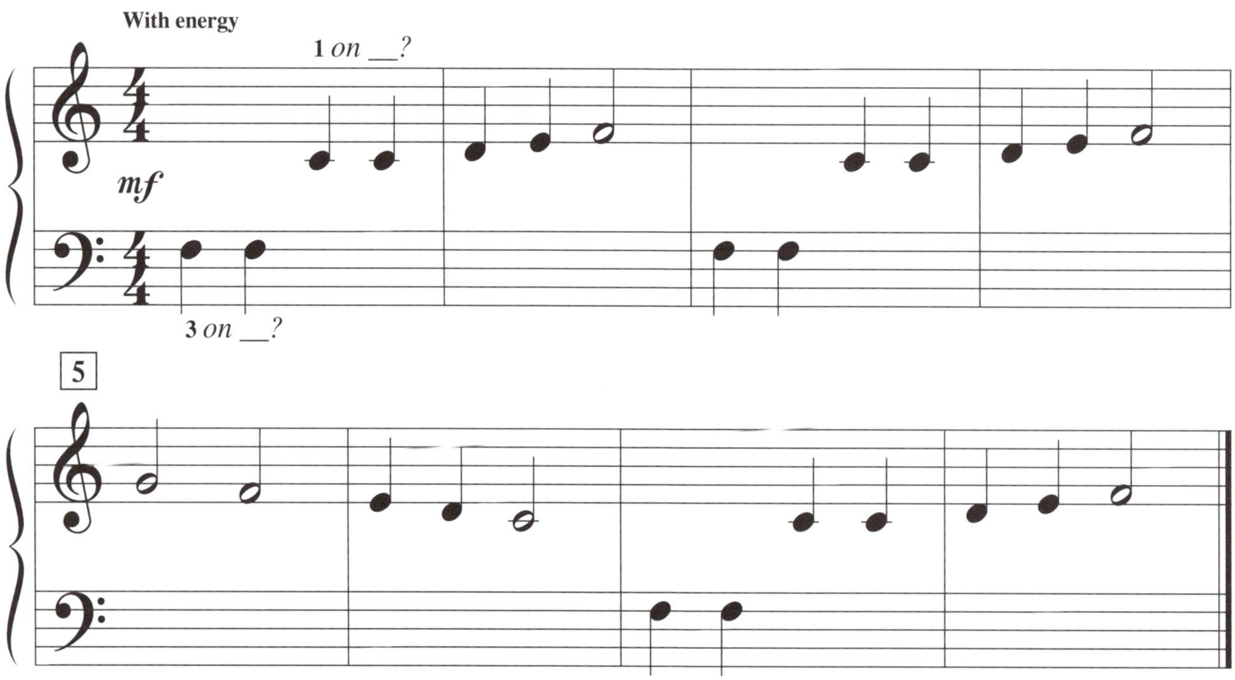

NOTE NAMES AND REPEATED NOTES

11. Say the **note names** aloud for this piece.

12. Three measures have **repeated** notes. Name these measures.

13. Which measure begins on **Treble G**?

Playback!

C 5-Finger Scale

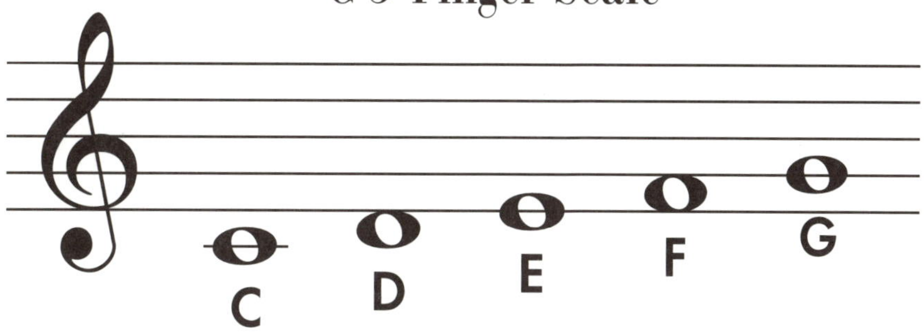

EAR-TRAINING "PLAYBACK"

14. Let's each place our R.H. in any **C 5-finger scale**.
    I'll always start on Middle C and play a few notes.
    You play back what you hear. (Sample examples)

C C D __	**C D E E**	**C D E F G __**	**C _ D _ E F G _**

IT'S TROPHY TIME FOR FROG TALK!

Frogs on Logs

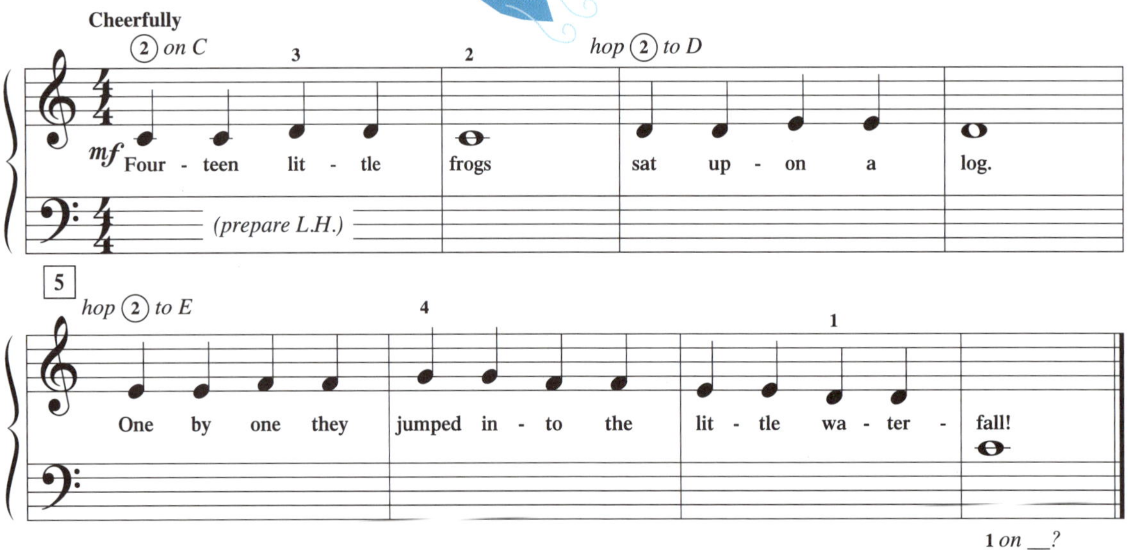

ADVENTURE CHALLENGE

- Can you name all the notes aloud in measures 5-8 for "Frogs on Logs?"
- Let's have a frog conversation!
  I'll play two notes with my R.H. and say **"RIB - BIT!"** (Ex. C-D)
  You answer me with your own **"RIB - BIT."**
  Let's try 3 **RIBBITS** back and forth.

FOR FUN!
Can you find a hidden treble clef and bass clef?

Can you find a hidden double bar line?

CONGRATULATIONS

YOU EARNED THE 5TH FUN STAR!

END OF THE UNIT 5 ASSESSMENT

UNIT 6 ASSESSMENT: Middle C B A G F Notes

Pages 56-63

NOTE READING AND RHYTHM REVIEW

1. Name this note. Is it a **line** or **space** note? Is it a *step* above or below **Middle C**? Play the rhythm and count aloud.

TECHNIQUE: FINGER CHANGES

2. Play this note with **L.H.** finger **1**, then finger **2**, then finger **3**.

3 means ____ beats in a measure

4 means the ____ note gets 1 beat

1

2

RHYTHM

3. What are the 2 numbers above called?
   Complete the definition by answering the blanks.

NAMING TIME SIGNATURES

4. Name the time signature for each example: $\frac{3}{4}$ or $\frac{4}{4}$

Show What you Know

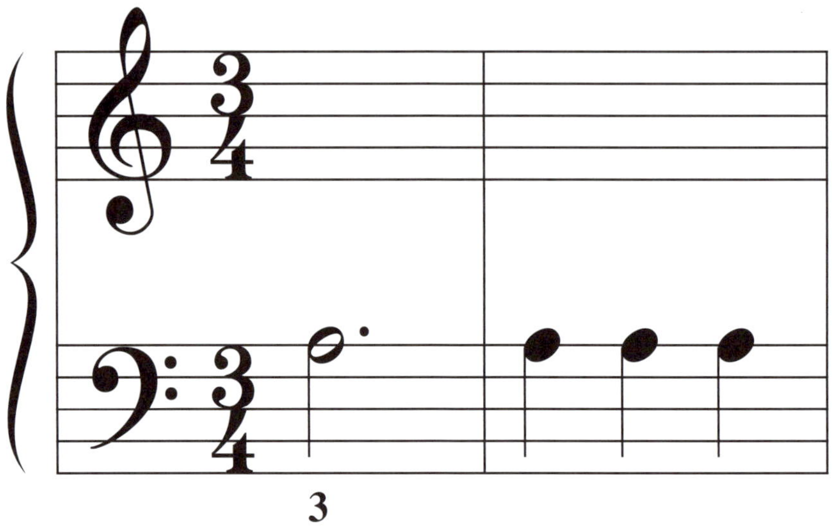

NOTE NAMES AND RHYTHM REVIEW

5. Name this note. Is it a **line** or **space** note? Is it a *step* or *skip* below Middle C? Play the rhythm and count aloud.

CREATIVE

6. Hold the pedal down and play all the **A**'s on the keyboard, LOW to HIGH. Make the final note the **A** shown above. (The teacher may demonstrate.)

Pattern Play

MEMORIZE WITH PATTERNS

7. First name the notes aloud.
   Which **2 measures** have the *same* pattern? How do the notes move?
   Look at **measure 3**. How do the notes move here?

8. Now find the **L.H. position**. Take a moment to silently look at the music.
   - First play while you are looking at the music.
   - Now try the tune by MEMORY, just by knowing the patterns!

NOTE NAMES AND RHYTHM REVIEW

9. Name this note. Is it a **line** or **space** note?
   Play the rhythm and count aloud.

TECHNIQUE

10. Play this note with **L.H.** finger **4**, then **3**, then **2**, then **1**.

1 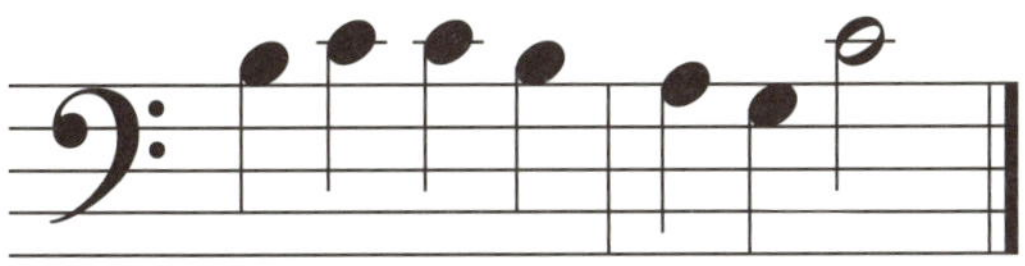

2 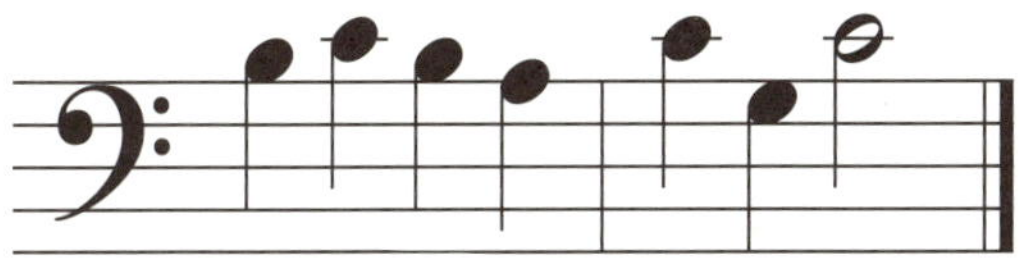

3 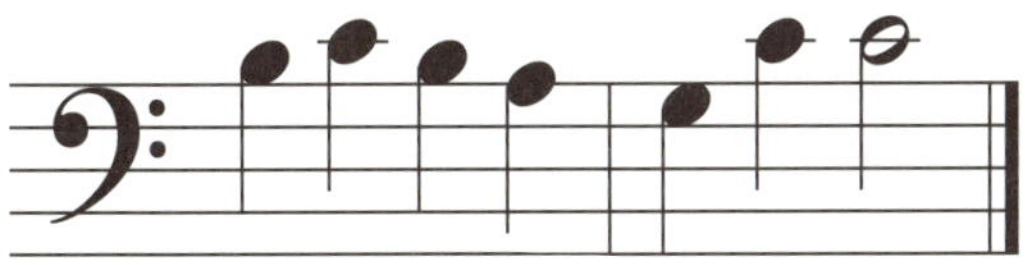

4 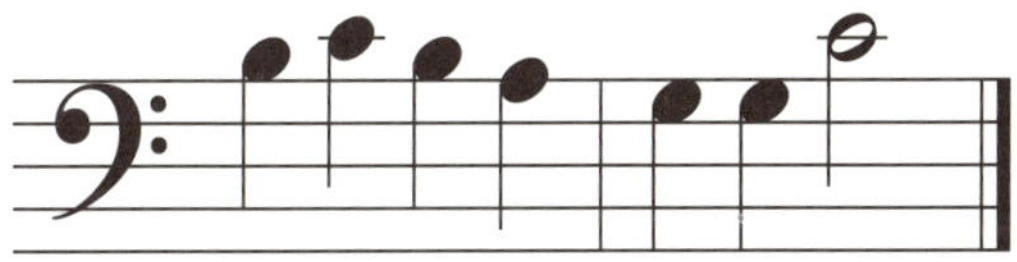

PATTERN RECOGNITION

11. Study the pattern at the top. Which pattern is an **exact match**?

EAR-TRAINING

12. I'll play pattern **1** or pattern **2**. Which did I play?
Repeat with patterns **3** and **4**.

Show What you Know

TROPHY WANTS YOU TO BE THE LEADER!

Come See the Parade!

ADVENTURE CHALLENGE

- I'll play line **1**, **2**, **3**, or **4** of the piece. Watch the music! Which line did I play?
- Play a line of music for me to guess. You're the leader!

FOR FUN!

Can you find a hidden half note?

Can you find a hidden *mf* sign?

CONGRATULATIONS

YOU'VE EARNED 6 SUPER STARS!

END OF THE UNIT 6 ASSESSMENT

Show What you Know

A skip moves

from a

line to a ___?___

or a

space to a ___?___.

READING BASICS

1. Complete the musical sentence.
   Can you say it by **memory**?

1

2

3

4

5

6

PATTERNS WITH SKIPS

2. Identify all the patterns that use a **skip**. Hint: There are four.
Let's do ear-training! I'll play pattern **1** or **2**. Which did you hear? (Continue with others.)

Show What you Know

TROPHY'S MUSICAL SKIPS!

New Position

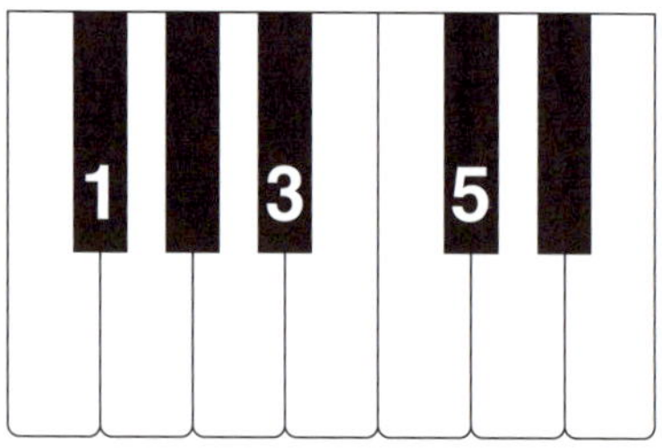

Hey, Hey, Look at Me!

ADVENTURE CHALLENGE

- Which measure has only half notes? Which has only quarter notes?
- Tap and count the rhythm aloud.
- We can play this song on the **black keys**. The keyboard will help you find the keys. (Coach as needed.)
- I'll go first and play in the new position. (Sing finger numbers.) Now it's your turn!

FOR FUN!

Can you find a hidden single staff?

Can you find a hidden grand staff?

CONGRATULATIONS

YOU'VE EARNED 7 COLORFUL STARS!

END OF THE UNIT 7 ASSESSMENT

UNIT 8 ASSESSMENT: Bass C D E F G Notes

Show What you Know

Pages 68-77

NEW NOTE NAME

1. Can you answer the rhyme, "Hey diddle diddle, what note's in the middle?"

REVIEW OF RHYTHM VALUES

2. The **1st** note is a whole note. How many beats?
   - What kind of note is the **2nd** note? How many beats?
   - What kind of note is the **3rd** note? How many beats?
   - And the **4th** note? How many beats?

NEW NOTE NAME AND RHYTHM REVIEW

3. Name the first note. What **space** is it on? Is the stem *up* or *down*?
Now name all the notes. Next, tap the rhythm. Last, play it for me on the piano!

TECHNIQUE: FINGER CHANGES

4. Play Bass **C** with **L.H.** finger **5**, then **4**, then **3**, then **2**, then **1**.

1

2

EAR-TRAINING

5. I'll play example **1** or **2**. Which one did I play?

6. Choose one and play it for me to name!

Steps, Skips, or Both?

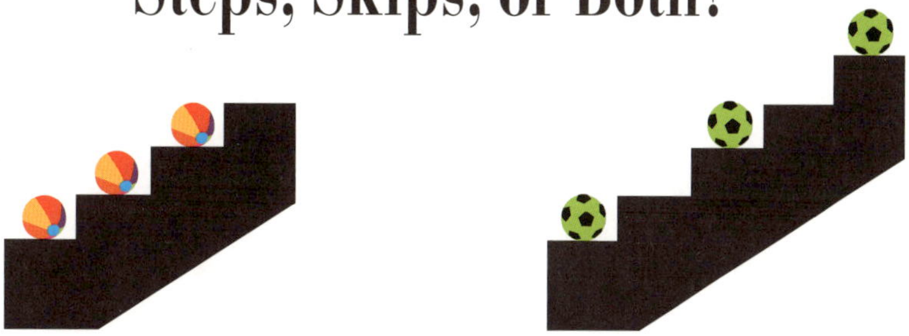

1
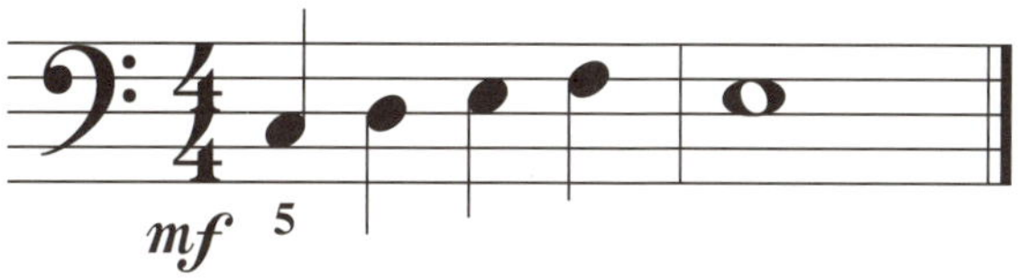

2

3

4

READING BY STEP AND SKIP

7. Does example **1** move by **steps**, **skips**, or **both**? How about example **2**? (Continue)

EAR-TRAINING

8. I'll play example **1**, **2**, **3**, or **4**. Which one did I play? Choose one to play for me!

Show What you Know

An octave is the distance of ____?____ notes.

THE OCTAVE

9. Complete the musical sentence.

PLAYING AN OCTAVE

10. Play **Middle C** with your **R.H.** and then the C one octave *higher*.
    Play **Bass C** with your **L.H.** and then the C one octave *lower*.

Purple Cat's Pattern

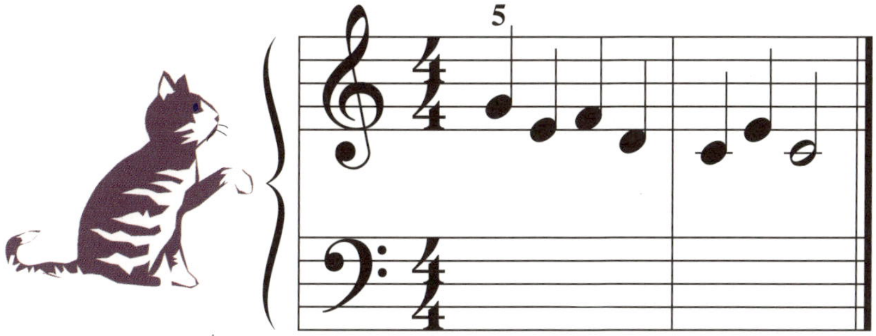

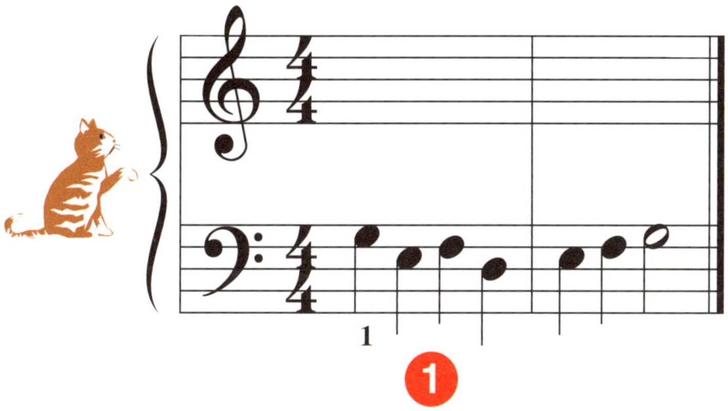

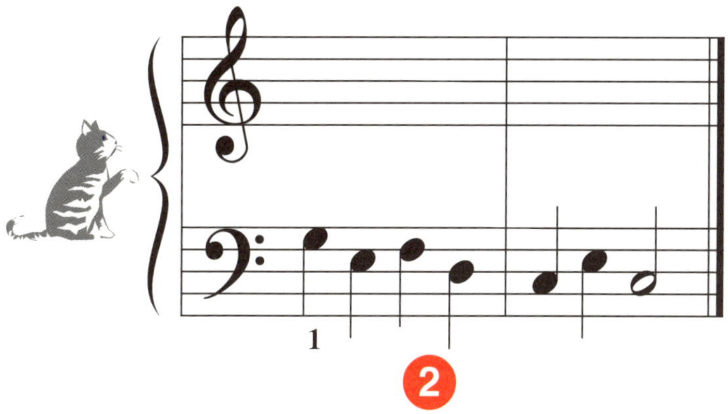

PATTERN IMITATION

11. Study the **Purple Cat's Pattern** of *steps* and *skips*.
    Is the perfect copycat pattern example **1** or **2**?

RHYTHM

12. Tap the rhythm of **Purple Cat's Pattern**.

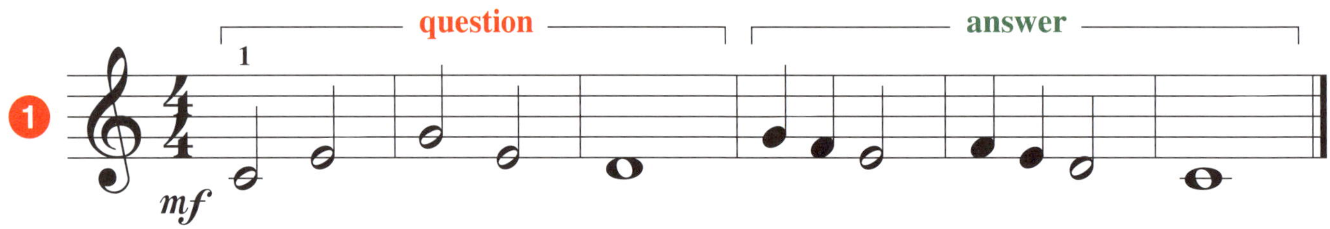

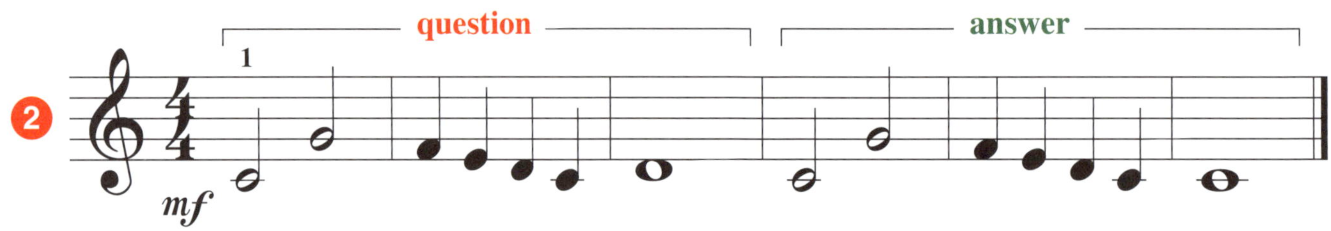

QUESTIONS AND ANSWERS

13. Does example **1** have a **parallel** or **contrasting** answer? Why? How about example **2**? Why?

SIGHTREADING

14. Play these **questions** and **answers** for your teacher. Remember to hold the half notes 2 beats!

CREATING ANSWERS

15. Your teacher will play the **question**. Can you play a **parallel answer**?
Your teacher will play the **question**. Can you play a **contrasting answer**?

Show What you Know

TROPHY ENJOYS PIE AND CAKE!

Grandmother

Question and Answer Song

Cheerfully

Traditional lyric adapted

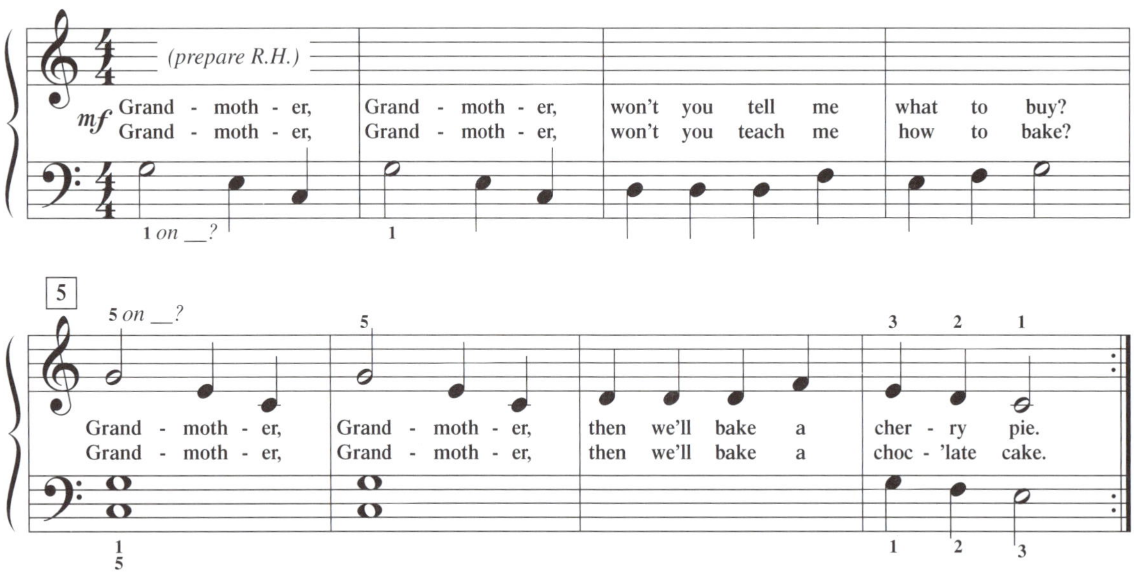

ADVENTURE CHALLENGE

- Only 2 measures in this piece move by STEPS. Find and name these 2 measures.
- Can you play the first 2 measures with your eyes closed?
- What do you like better—cherry pie or chocolate cake?

FOR FUN!

Can you find the word "octave" hidden above?

Can you find this hidden pattern above? 

CONGRATULATIONS

YOU'VE EARNED 8 GREAT STARS!

END OF THE UNIT 8 ASSESSMENT

UNIT 9 ASSESSMENT: The Tie

Pages 78-81

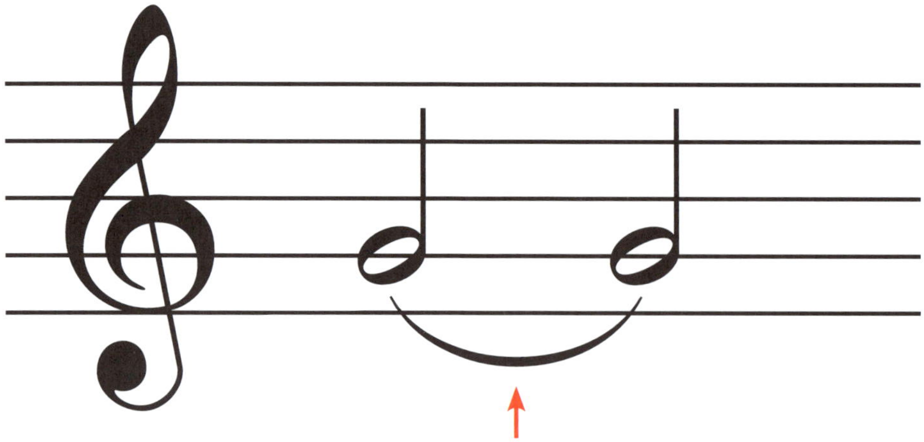

1

2

3

SYMBOLS

1. What is the curved line at the top of the page? What is the **total number of beats**?

RHYTHM

2. Now name the **total beats** for each of the **tied** notes in the boxes.

Rhythm Taps!

1

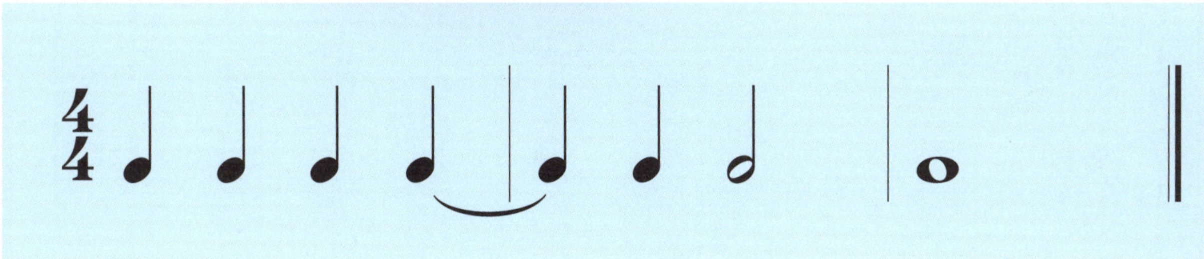

2

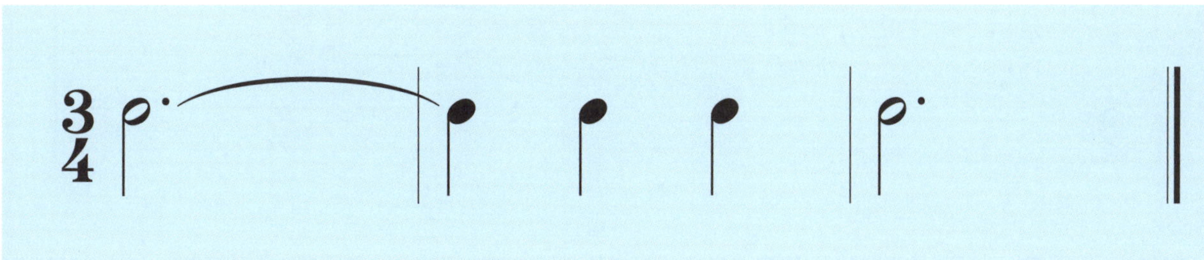

TAPPING RHYTHMS WITH TIES

3. Take a moment to study rhythm **1**. Where is the **tie**?
   Tap with your **R.H.** on the closed key cover. (The teacher may join.)

4. Now study rhythm **2**. Where is the **tie**?
   Tap with your **L.H.** on the closed key cover.

Show What you Know

TROPHY RINGS CHIMES WITH BIG BEN!

Bells of Great Britain

______ 5-Finger Scale

Joyfully, with steady gongs

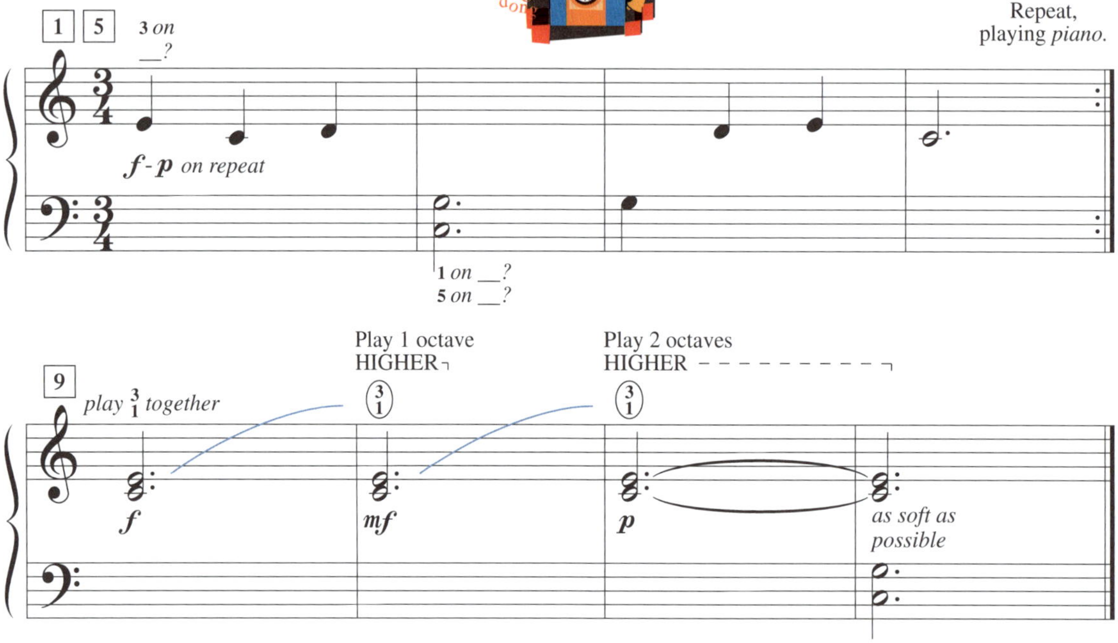

ADVENTURE CHALLENGE

- In which 2 measures does the L.H. play **fingers 1** and **5 together**?
- Hold the pedal down. Play **skips** with **R.H. fingers 2** and **4** HIGH on the keys. I'll go first. (Play a short example.) Now it's your turn!

FOR FUN!

Can you find 2 hidden ties above?

How many total beats for each?

CONGRATULATIONS

YOU'VE EARNED 9 MUSICAL STARS!

END OF THE UNIT 9 ASSESSMENT

UNIT 10 ASSESSMENT: The Quarter Rest

Pages 82-87

SYMBOLS

1. What is this symbol? What does it mean to do?

2. How many of these would equal a **whole note**?
   How many would equal a **half note**?

RHYTHM

3. Notice the time signature. These measures are *incomplete*.
   How many **quarter rests** are needed to:

   • complete measure **1**? • complete measure **2**? • complete measure **3**?

Show What you Know

TAPPING RHYTHMS WITH QUARTER RESTS

4. Check each measure. Is this rhythm now correct? Let's tap it together. We'll clap for the notes and *open our hands* for the quarter rests.

Ex. 1 1 1 rest | 1-2 rest rest | 1 rest rest rest ||

RHYTHMS WITH QUARTER RESTS

1

2

3

4

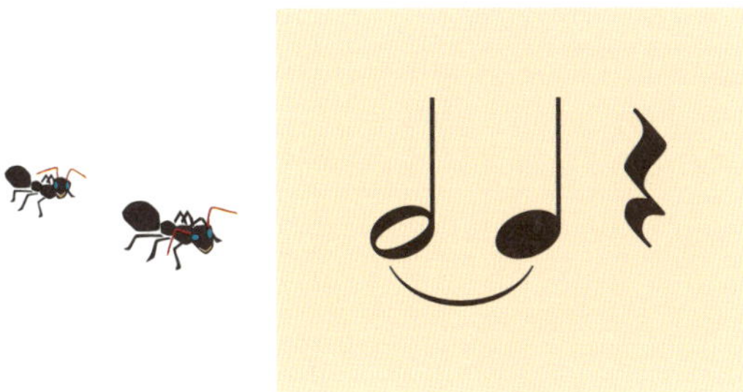

5

6

RHYTHM: COUNTING THE BEATS

5. Only three examples have exactly **4 beats**.
   Can you name them?

6. Which two examples have **3 beats**?

TROPHY'S VARIATION OF THE BUGLE BOYS!

FINAL ADVENTURE CHALLENGE

- In Trophy's Variation, the **R.H.** plays the Introduction. The **L.H.** plays the melody! I'll play it for you first. Watch and listen! Then you sightread it for me.

FOR FUN!
Can you find 3 hidden quarter rests above?

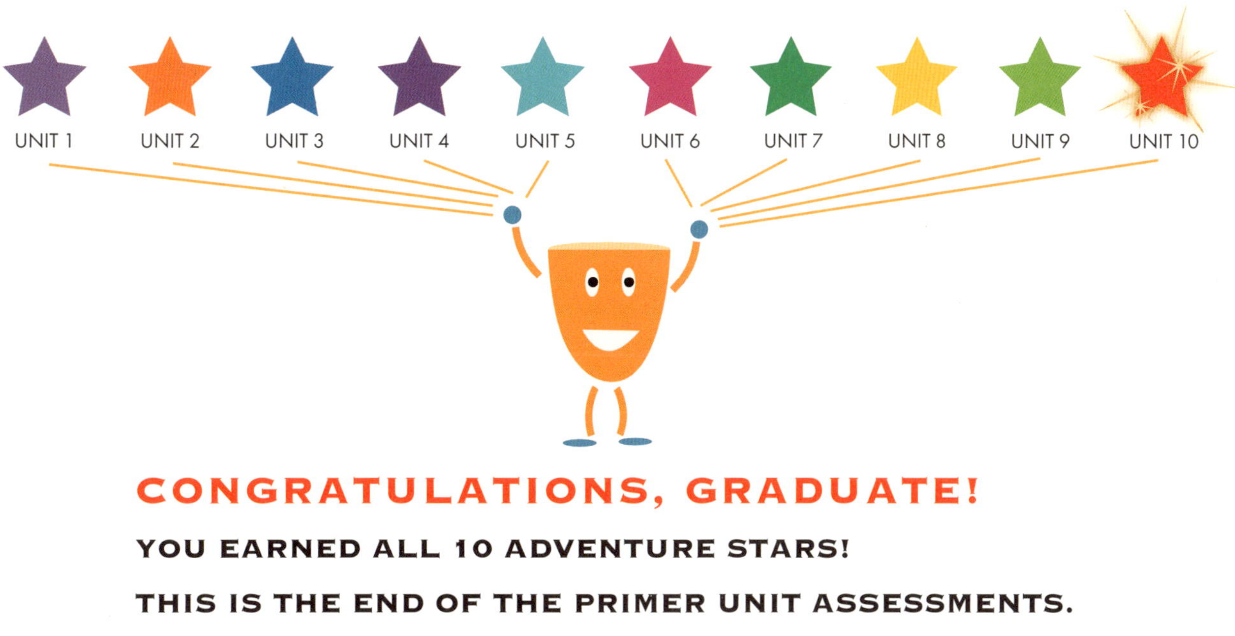

CONGRATULATIONS, GRADUATE!

YOU EARNED ALL 10 ADVENTURE STARS!

THIS IS THE END OF THE PRIMER UNIT ASSESSMENTS.

Assess for Success!

YOU ARE NOW READY FOR LEVEL 1 BOOKS

Lesson

Theory

Technique & Artistry

Performance

Sightreading

Some instructors teaching 30-minute lessons may prefer using the Sightreading Book instead of the Performance Book.

FABER
PIANO ADVENTURES®